MYS

OF
THE KEYS
OF THE
KINGDOM

JESUS'S GIFT FOR
A LIFE OF VICTORY

Karie

The Keys in this book
can make the difference
between just existing and
living a life of victory

Enjoy

DEBORAH BOUCHARD

Deborah

Printed in the United States of America

ISBN: Softcover   978-1-63871-676-1
          Hardback   978-1-63871-659-4
          eBook   978-1-63871-660-0

Republished by: PageTurner Press and Media LLC
Publication Date: 10/26/2021

To order copies of this book, contact:
PageTurner Press and Media
Phone: 1-888-447-9651
info@pageturner.us
www.pageturner.us

ALL BIBLE REFERENCES ARE TAKEN FROM:

- *New King James Version Spirit Filled Life Bible*, Thomas Nelson Publishers, Nashville, copyright 1991 by Thomas Nelson, Inc.

- *The New Strong's Exhaustive Concordance of the Bible*, copyright 1995 by Thomas Nelson Inc.

- *The Power of the Blood Covenant, Uncover the Secret Strength in God's Eternal Oath* by Malcolm Smith, copyright 2002, Harrison House Publishers

- Rockofoffence.com/mysts.html

- *Unraveling the Mystery of the Blood Covenant* by John Osteen, copyright January 1987 Osteen Publications, John

- *The Name of Jesus* by Kenneth E. Hagin, copyright 2006 RHEMA Bible Church

- *The Believer's Authority* by Kenneth E. Hagin, copyright 2004 RHEMA Bible Church

CONTENTS

Prologue

"Father, what is that in your hand?" asked three-year-old Jacob.

"Well, son, these are keys. They open locks."

"Like this chest?" Jacob asked inquisitively as he pointed to the chest on the table. Father reached over to the chest and picked it up.

"You see this lock?" Little Jacob nodded.

"Inside are very important things that I don't want just anybody to see," the father continued. "When I am ready to take something out of the chest, I have to use this key to open it. Do you understand?" Jacob nodded, but then asked, "But you have many keys in your hand. Does it take all those keys to unlock this chest?"

Father chuckled and picked up his young son. "No, Jacob. There are many locks in this house that need keys. The lock on this chest has its key. See this door? It has its own key. Each key has a specific lock that it opens."

Father set Jacob down and knelt down beside him. "One day, you will hold many keys in your hands and you will have access to many locked doors and chests. Anyone who holds those keys and knows which door or lock it will open will have access into the house or room or chest or car or anything that needs a lock."

Jacob looked content with his father's explanation. Then he asked, "Father, can I have some keys to hold? I want to use them to get into my playhouse."

When Jesus came into the region of Caesarea Philippi, He asked His disciples saying, "Who do men say that I, the Son of Man, am?"

Simon Peter answered and said, "You are the Christ, the Son of the living God."

Jesus answered and said to him, "Blessed are you, Simon Bar-Jonah, for flesh and blood has not revealed this to you, but My Father who is in heaven. And I also say to you that you are Peter and on this rock I will build My church and the gates of Hades shall not prevail against it. And I will give you the keys of the kingdom of heaven and whatever you bind on earth, will be bound in heaven, and whatever you loose on earth will be loosed in heaven."

—Matthew 16:13, 16–19

Chapter 1

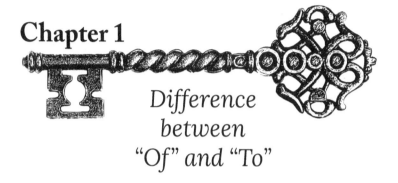

Difference between "Of" and "To"

The title of this book is *Mystery of the Keys* of *the Kingdom.* The Lord showed me the difference between the little words "to" and "of." The word "to" the Kingdom means a way, a door, the gate to the Kingdom of Heaven.

Jesus clearly explained that He is the way. "I am the Way, the Truth and the Life. No one comes to the Father but through Me" (John 14:6). Or "I am the door. If anyone enters by Me, he will be saved and will go in and out and find pasture" (John 10:7, 8).

The word "to" the Kingdom of Heaven refers to Jesus Christ. When you accept Him as the Son of God and understand that Jesus was born of the virgin Mary; lived a life on the earth showing and sharing the love of God through signs and miracles; died on the cross for our sins, sickness, and torments; rose on the third day; and now sits at the right hand of God the Father, you will be saved and spend eternity with Jesus in the heavenly Kingdom that God has set up for us.

*"And I will give you the keys **of** the kingdom of heaven and whatever you bind on earth will be bound in heaven, and whatever you loose on earth will be loosed in heaven."* (Matthew 16:19)

The word *"of "* the Kingdom of Heaven is quite different. It reveals access to a life of victory because of what Jesus the Christ, the Messiah, accomplished when He allowed the Pharisees and Roman soldiers to apprehend Him and take Him to the cross.

Let me take you to a scene in the book of Matthew 16 that reveals the transfer of the Keys to mankind. Jesus was in Caesarea Philippi which was a Roman city in the very northern tip of Israel. He had his disciples around Him, probably resting along the roadside.

They had been having conversations about the hypocrisy of the Pharisees who would act and proclaim how pure they were, but in reality, there were ulterior motives, deceit, bribery, sexual immorality, and on and on among the lives of the so-called Holy Men. So Jesus was explaining the illustration of yeast in dough that grows to make a loaf of bread is like the sin among the Pharisees that continues to grow among them (Matthew 16:5–12).

Then, He asks the disciples, "Who do men say that I, the Son of Man, am?" A few of the disciples offered an answer, saying, "Some say John the Baptist, some Elijah, and others Jeremiah or one of the prophets."

Jesus then turns the question on them and asks, "But who do you say that I am?" I'm sure the disciples looked at each other or stared at the ground thinking when Peter blurts out, "You are the Christ, the Son of the living God."

Jesus focused on Peter a moment, then said, "Blessed are you, Simon Bar-Jonah, for flesh and blood has not revealed this to you, but My Father who is in heaven. And I also say to you that you are Peter," as Jesus placed his hand on Peter's shoulder, "and on this rock, I will build My church and the gates of Hades shall not prevail against it. And I will give you the keys **of** the Kingdom of Heaven and whatever you bind on earth will be bound in heaven, and whatever you loose on earth will be loosed in heaven" (Matthew 16:13–19).

There are so many important messages in what Jesus just told Peter with the disciples looking on. First of all, Peter may have only thought around the edges of the fact that Jesus was truly the Son of God as he listened to Jesus teach, but at this very moment, the realization dropped from his head into his heart. Peter was, at that moment, convinced that Jesus was truly the long-awaited Messiah.

Second, Jesus declared that Peter would be the beginning of the Church. No one had ever heard of "church" since it was always the temple or synagogue. At that very moment, with the words spoken into the atmosphere, Jesus was launching the establishment of the Church.

Also, at that moment in time, something had been established in the natural and supernatural worlds and even Satan and his kingdom would never defeat it. "And the gates of Hades shall not prevail against it." Then Jesus decreed that He was giving Peter the keys of the Kingdom of Heaven that would give the power and authority to make declarations to bind and loose what God has made available to not only Peter, but to all those who acknowledge, believe and are convinced the Jesus was passing His authority to them (Matthew 16:1–19).

It is especially important to realize that this "doctrine" did not fade or weaken in power or authority when Jesus passed from this earth to heaven or when the last of the apostles died. This new "law" was established for all people who were born or to be born in years and centuries beyond. All of mankind were given permission to exert their authority over strategies and maneuvers from the underworld which is in Satan's control.

To confirm this, in John 16, Jesus is speaking to the disciples in his last week on the earth before His crucifixion. He explained that He must leave the earth and go away so the Helper would come. The Helper refers to the Holy Spirit who would come to guide believers into all truth. Jesus said, *"He will guide you into all truth for He will not speak on His own authority but whatever He hears He will speak, and He will tell you things to come. He will glorify Me, for He will take of what is Mine and declare it to you. All things that the Father has are Mine. Therefore, I said that He will take of Mine and declare it to you"* (John 16:13–15).

Christ Jesus (who was God wrapped in humanity) came to bring the Kingdom of Heaven back to the earth. He restored the power and authority of the Kingdom through His death and resurrection, defeating Satan, and now He is making it possible to continue that same power and authority for us to use as believers. It will be the Holy Spirit that makes it possible as I will discuss in following chapters.

Finally, those who believe in the Good News of the gospel of Jesus Christ has been given legal authority to do and say what Jesus did as He walked the earth. Jesus Himself was transferring all that He had to those of us who are believers (vs. 15).

The apostle Paul, who had a very dynamic understanding of this told us in Romans 8:16 & 17; *"The Spirit Himself bears witness with our spirit that we are children of God, and if children, then heirs— heirs of God and joint heirs with Christ."*

Being an heir is a legal term that gives us all the rights, privileges, and authority of the one who names us their heir. We are joint heirs with Christ! What He has, we have; the authority

He carried from His Father, we have that same authority! This is great news for those of us who have been hammered down by life. Satan's plan for us is to kill our dreams and aspirations; steal our peace and joy; and destroy our lives with fear, sickness, and disease. But Jesus's plan is to give us life more than we could ever imagine. His gift of life is to make continual progress and experience success in our life. We are not to live a life of just "hanging on," or barely getting by but to experience the joy of life, peace that no one would understand because we are His and carry incredible power and authority through simply making Him our Lord and Savior.

So let's find out what those Keys **of** the Kingdom are. You won't be disappointed, and I'm sure it will open a whole new idea of exactly who you are in Jesus Christ and the power you carry over the spirit realm.

Chapter 2

Key #1

Our Covenant

Dr. David Livingstone was a physician, missionary, and staunch abolitionist in the mid-1800s. He decided to explore the "dark continent" of Africa to find the source of the Nile River and expose the plight of the Africans who were being enslaved by slave traffickers. Although it was supposed to be a two-year expedition, it had been almost six years since anyone had heard from Dr. Livingstone. Americans were intrigued with his progress, especially the editor of the *New York Herald*, James. G. Bennett Jr.

A journalist by the name of Henry M. Stanley was already in Africa working for the *Herald* and was now being assigned to find the missing Dr. Livingstone. He willingly started on his journey with hundreds of porters and guides carrying multitudes of supplies and equipment to help make his life relatively comfortable. He also had numerous animals in the caravan, including a favorite goat that provided Henry with goat milk for his sensitive stomach.

The deeper the troupe moved into the jungles following the trail of Dr. Livingstone, the more challenges they faced. Tropical diseases decimated many of the porters and many others deserted. Animals died from bug bites and jungle beasts; nonetheless, many survived and continued.

Traveling through tribal territories became a challenge for the foreigners. Besides the difficult terrain, insects, and threat from wild animals, there is always a village or governed territory to pass through. Whenever a stranger enters a territory or village, there will be a challenge by the natives. On one such day, the exploration troupe needed to pass through the only way to their destination which covered thousands of acres of this tribal territory.

Stanley and his men were met by a group of warriors and taken to the chief. The amount of land and the many villages in this territory made this particular chief very powerful. When they came to the chief's village, Stanley's interpreter explained, pointing to the explorers, this group needed to cross the chief's land. The chief didn't know these people, and to get his permission, it was agreed that they had to make covenant. This would provide protection for the chief and his people and protection for Stanley and his men.

Covenant is a legally binding agreement between two parties. It was used often before there were attorneys that would write up documents that could be signed by both parties. In this case, to make the covenant, there had to be the shedding of blood between them. Stanley had the interpreter stand in for him and the chief's son stood in for him. The village joined in this ceremony, for it was a very serious and sobering one.

The first part of the ceremony was made up of promises or vows that could not be broken. Each party vowed to protect each other. That would mean if someone wanted to hurt or kill anyone in either the tribe or the exploration group, the other was bound to protect them or their honor. In other words, they had each other's back. They would stand up for each other. If one group was attacked, it was expected the other group would come to their defense. Then there were conditions to be kept. If either one broke their promise, then it is understood that the other group was free to kill the offending people.

Another part of the ceremony was a name exchange. They were legally allowed to use the other's name. The chief could use Stanley's name and Stanley could use the chief's name. This could possibly come at a time when their lives were threatened or a trade deal was necessary.

Following the name exchange, an item that was special to each participant was given to the other. The interpreter told Stanley that the chief wanted his goat. Stanley argued that the goat was necessary for his intestinal health. But the chief, seeing how valuable the goat was to Stanley, insisted on the goat. Stanley reluctantly agreed and waited to see what the chief would give him in exchange. To his dismay, all the chief produced was a large stick with some paint and copper wire wound around the stick. It was old and well-worn, and Stanley felt he got the raw end of the deal. However, as it was explained by the interpreter that the tokens exchanged was saying, "What is mine is yours and what is yours is mine."

Lastly, to seal the covenant, each representative cut their hand to draw blood. Then mixing their blood with milk, they drank the mixture. This ended the ceremony, creating a bond between the tribe and the travelers.

After spending the night, early the next morning, Stanley and his men started on their way. Still upset that he was leaving his goat, Stanley couldn't understand how this staff would benefit him. It didn't take long before he found out the power of the staff. As he approached each village, the warriors would confront them to protect their village. But when they saw the staff, they either invited them for a meal in their village or led them to the edge of their territory. In one village, they were so happy to have the American visitor that they gave him several of their goats. Stanley was amazed that because of the chief's identity in the staff, he received triple portion of what he gave up. As it turned out, the simple token the chief had given him yielded great power and authority throughout the rest of their trip.

Eventually, Henry Stanley found the missing Dr. David Livingstone who needed many of the goods that Henry carried through seven hundred miles of jungle.

Our Covenant with God

God cut covenant with many men in the Old Testament, notably with Abraham. He put Abraham to sleep, then divided an ox down the middle andwalked in the blood between the halves. As he did that, God gave Abraham a promise of prosperity and that he would be a great nation. God also promised that in Him through Jesus Christ, all the families of the earth were to be blessed (Gal 3:16; John 8:56–58) In the exchange, Abraham was told he had to circumcise all the males in his family and to continue to circumcise all males for all generations. So blood was drawn on both sides of the parties. As a result, God would have a covenant or binding contract with all Abraham's descendants throughout their generations (Genesis 17:10 & 11). God then created His laws and ordinances to be followed for God to protect, provide, and care for His people. In return, God expected obedience and worship from His chosen people.

In the New Testament, it was God and Jesus who cut covenant. Jesus was the one that was sacrificed on the cross for mankind and shed his blood. Jesus declared to his disciples at the last supper, *"This is My blood of the new covenant, which is shed for many for the remission of sins"* (Matthew 26:28). Jesus stood in for all people who lived in the past, his present, and all future generations. That includes you and me. Jesus became the mediator (the One that stands between) for us. Just as the chief's son and the interpreter did.

The shed blood of Jesus Christ did many things for us that we must understand. Just as Henry Stanley had exchanged vows with the chief, so have we made vows with God when we asked Him to be Lord of our lives.

In the covenant that was made with mankind, God put His laws in our minds and they are written on our hearts. For this is the covenant that I will make with the house of Israel after those days, says the Lord: I will put My laws in their mind and write them on their hearts; and I will be their God, and they shall be My people (Hebrews 8:10). Our conscience will tell us when we are doing the right thing or the wrong thing. We don't have to go by man's laws to understand the difference between right and wrong. We *know* because God has put them in our subconscious.

The Vow or Promise

Throughout the New Testament, unconditional blessing was based upon the finished redemption of Christ for all who would believe. In this truth, God is bound to protect, provide, heal, and encourage you. Our covenant through Jesus Christ secures blessing for the church body which flows from the Abrahamic covenant. It is unconditional, final, and irreversible. It is a binding contract and cannot be nullified.

The Condition of the Promise

If you remember in the case of Henry Stanley and the chief, if one of them broke their vow, then there were serious ramifications. There are also conditions in our covenant with God through Jesus Christ. God won't strike you dead or curse you if you break your covenant with Him. The whole Trinity, God the Father, the Son Jesus Christ, and the Holy Spirit are gentlemen. If we choose to dishonor the covenant we made with Him in our confession of faith, then our Father in heaven will simply neglect you. This is profoundly serious because once He lifts his protective covering off you, then you are vulnerable to all assaults from your mortal enemy, Satan. The neglect is a result of your choice to turn your back on your Savior. However, God never turns His back on you. His arms are always open to receive you back.

The Name Exchange

Remember, as the two representatives performed the covenant ceremony in the jungles of Africa, Stanley was given the chief's name to use and the chief received Stanley's name. This was beneficial for both parties as it made the way for protection and commerce. That is what happened when Jesus Christ was our representative with God. We received the name of Jesus Christ and He got our name. Our names were legally exchanged when we became a believer, a part of God's family. At this moment, our names are written in the Book of Life.

In one of the longest teaching sessions Jesus had with His disciples is in John 16. In verse 23, He said, *"And in that day, you will ask Me nothing. Most assuredly I say to you, whatever you ask the Father in My name He will give you. Until now you have asked nothing in My name. Ask and you will receive, that your joy may be full."*

Jesus gave us His name to use as authority in the spirit realm. In Philippians 2:10–11, Paul wrote, *"At the name of Jesus, every knee shall bow, those beings above the earth (angels), on the earth (people), and under the earth (demons), and every tongue shall confess that Jesus Christ is Lord to the glory of God the Father."* Jesus wants us to use His name. In John 14:12, He said, *"Most assuredly, I say to you, he who believes in Me, the works that I do he will do also; and greater works than these he will do, because I go to My Father. And whatever you ask in My name, that I will do, that the Father may be glorified in the Son. If you ask anything in My name, I will do it."*

Without a doubt, there is great power when we use Jesus's name to advance the kingdom of God.

The Possessions

One of the most amazing part about the story of Stanley and the chief is the exchange of possessions. Stanley had to give up his precious goat and got a stick with copper and paint on it. It wasn't until Stanley and his men needed to pass through villages that he realized the power of authority that he held. That stick represented the chief who all the villages honored. By holding that stick, Stanley himself received the same honor.

As a believer, you can hold a "stick" over Jesus's and our enemy, Satan. Jesus passed His symbol of authority on to us. The following gifts or possessions are ours to use: first of all, our salvation, then the Holy Spirit, Peace, and Love.

The Holy Spirit

Through our belief of Jesus Christ as our Lord and Savior, we have received many gifts. First is the gift of salvation which means all our sins have been forgiven and we can start a whole new life. But we can't start a whole new life without help, so we are also given the gift of the Holy Spirit. The Holy Spirit is the one who will guide us into all Truth. John 16:13 says *"However, when He the Spirit of Truth has come, He will guide you into all truth for He will not speak on His own authority, but whatever He hears He will speak; and He will tell you things to come."* We don't necessarily "feel" the Holy Spirit as He abides in us, but we hear Him in our inner being. That quiet voice that will instruct you as you face different situations from day to day.

Peace

As a child of the Creator of the Universe, who is also our Lord, He is now responsible for your protection, health, guidance, and provision. There should be no fretting, no worry, no anxiety. Only a sense of peace that your life is in the hands of your heavenly Father who wants the best for you. Jesus said in John 14:27, *"Peace I leave with you. My peace I give to you, not as the world gives do I give to you. Let not your heart be troubled, neither let it be afraid."*

Then in John 16:33, Jesus again says, *"These things I have spoken to you, that in Me you may have peace. In the world you will have tribulation but be of good cheer, I have overcome the world."*

Both times, Jesus is emphasizing that the world will *not* give you peace. That the only way to live in peace is to trust in your Savior Jesus Christ. Trust that He will be there in your crisis and hold you. Trust that He will make provision for whatever you need. Trust that He will protect you in the dark of the night. Trust that healing is yours. Trust in His name!

He Also Gave Us Love

There is an incredible transference when we start our new life with Jesus as the Lord of our life. There is an infilling of love that no one can explain. Let it flood your life. Open your eyes and heart to see people as Jesus sees people. There may be someone in your life that is hard to deal with, maybe unloveable, but we don't know who or what circumstances made them that way. Just know that Jesus died for them as well and loves them just as He loves you. Jesus said in John 15:12. *"This is my commandment, that you love one another as I have loved you."* Loving the unlovable will take time, but with the infilling and inspiration from the Holy Spirit and perhaps other believers, you will find yourself changed.

Results of Being in Covenant with the Most High God

Believe it or not, we are in covenant (a binding legal agreement) with the same God who made the universe: the stars, sun, and moon, the birds of the air, and the fish of the sea. When we understand and accept that, then we know we have a powerful, good and trustworthy Father who has our back. There is great security in that understanding.

He has given us so much: the Holy Spirit, peace, love, joy, and confident assurance that we are not going through life's journey alone. The author of Hebrews reminds us that God Himself said, "I will never leave or forsake you" (Heb. 13:5). This means, God (Jesus) will in no circumstance let up or slacken His hold on you or leave you behind in some place to fend for yourself. He is in partnership with you in this life.

In return, we must obey His voice and be able to act quickly in response to that voice. Act like Jesus or be Jesus in skin. Just doing little things like picking up trash in the parking lot, helping someone struggling with their children or groceries would be pleasing to God. Do you feel a nudge to give a financial gift to someone or some institution? Then give your very best. If someone asks you to pray for them, do it right then. Don't wait. We should respond to His voice to help others everywhere we go. There are many opportunities that the Holy Spirit gives, and we need to step out of our comfort zone and obey God. We must not make our own agenda but walk out His agenda for us.

Being in covenant means we must defend Him. Stand up for His principles and commandments even if it takes a little of your money or time and even get backlash from the world. We must walk through each day, knowing we have a covenant with the King of the world. He has your back and we must have His back.

Many church folks are timid to stand up for Jesus and His principles. Many are afraid of being shouted down. We are in the season that God is opening up opportunities to be His voice and His hands and feet. There is nothing to be embarrassed about. He died for you and me, so we can share His story of love and forgiveness for our wickedness that separated us from God. His sacrifice on the cross bridged that gap, so we can be in constant communion with our Father in heaven, our Covenant Maker.

So the first key of the Kingdom which we receive from our commitment to the King of all kings and the Lord of all lords is being in covenant, a legally binding contract with our Father in Heaven, God.

Chapter 3

Key #2

The Baptism of
the Holy Spirit

To begin this second key, we have to ask, "Who is the Holy Spirit?" I have already mentioned that the Holy Spirit is a gift. We don't earn the Holy Spirit. He is ours to receive. If your parent would hand you a beautifully wrapped box with a bow and extended their hands with box in it to you, would you just stand there with your hands at your side? No! You would reach out to receive the gift. That is what God and Jesus want you to do. This is Their gift to you. In this gift of the Holy Spirit are many parts that we will explore.

The Holy Spirit Is a Real Person

First of all, know that the Holy Spirit is not an "It." He is a person. He has feelings. He can be excited, He has a personality, and enjoys making you happy. He has a sense of humor, but most of all, He is your friend. The Holy Spirit is a gentleman, kind, and patient. However, His feelings can be hurt and offended. To deny that the Holy Spirit exists and is available to us as an agent of Heaven is the greatest offense of all. The Holy Spirit is part of the Holy Trinity.

To explain the Holy Trinity, I will put it this way: God is the Brain, the visionary; Jesus is the Mouth, and the Holy Spirit are the Hands. A great example is in Genesis 1. God comes up with the idea of creating the earth (Genesis 1:1). Jesus spoke it into existence (John 1:1) and the Holy Spirit carried it out (Genesis 1:2). They are all One for when the Bible says, "God said," they are all a part of creation.

Another illustration of how the Trinity can be explained is through water. Water placed in a small pot and placed in a freezer will freeze. Take that pot and place it over a fire, it will melt and become water. Leave it on the stove long enough, it will begin to boil which will produce steam. It's all the same water, but in three different forms: hard, liquid, and steam.

Who is the Holy Spirit? He is the heavenly agent that is part of the Godhead sent to us on earth to be everywhere, with everyone. He was released to the world when Jesus re-entered heaven after His resurrection. The Holy Spirit is the one who will teach you God's principles, guide you in your decisions and council you as you walk through the rest of your life. Once a person believes in Jesus Christ, who lived, died, was raised supernaturally from the dead and now is in Heaven ruling with God, then the Holy Spirit is sent to live on the inside of that person. *And I will pray the Father, and He will give you another Helper, that He may abide with you forever—the Spirit of Truth, whom the world cannot receive, because it neither sees Him nor knows Him; but you know Him, for He dwells with you and will be in you* (John

14:16, 17). It is a supernatural event. You are the same person, same personality, same family, but something is different in your heart. You will start to think and perceive differently and have different desires.

The disciples experienced this supernatural event. In John 20:19–23, the apostles were in hiding right after their revered teacher, Jesus, was crucified. They feared the authorities would find them and do the same to them as they did to Jesus. As the eleven of Jesus's closest friends were discussing their situation, Jesus suddenly appeared in the room and said to them, *"Peace be with you."* To prove it was really Him, He showed the wounds in His hands, feet, and side. Once the disciples were convinced it was truly Jesus, they rejoiced and were glad to see their Lord.

Jesus said to them again, *"Peace to you! As the Father has sent Me, I also send you." At that moment, Jesus breathed on them and said, "Receive the Holy Spirit"* (John 20:20). Because they were witnesses, the disciples knew Jesus had risen from the dead and were convinced that He was the long-awaited Messiah. When Jesus "breathed on them," they were receiving the initial infilling of the Holy Spirit supernaturally, just as you and I receive when we believe and receive Him as our Lord and Savior. From that moment on, the disciples were what we now call Christians.

We are baptized into the family of God, known as children of God. The word *baptize* in the Greek is *baptizo* which means to be immersed or to make overwhelmed. I will be explaining the three baptisms in this chapter. The first baptism a person experiences is when we accept Jesus as the Messiah, the Son of God. At that time, we are immediately baptized into the family of God.

When we become believers in Jesus Christ, there will be a desire to know more about Him, His message, and the future that God has established for us. The Holy Spirit will help you change thought patterns, habits, attitudes, and even traditions that aren't pleasing to God. If it is your heart's desire to please God, you will receive the gentle nudging of the Holy Spirit.

One of the characteristics of God is in His name Jehovah Shammah. He is the Lord that will never leave you. That is the Holy Spirit who is with you always. He will teach, guide, council, and direct your thoughts. That is a good thing! You will become a changed (for the better) person and all your thoughts will be lining up with what Jesus would be pleased with. Paul explained, *"If anyone is in Christ he is a new creation; old things have passed away; behold all things have become new"* (2 Cor. 5:18).

You should have a hunger to know more about God, the life of Jesus, and what He has for you. You can find all of this in His Word, the Bible. If you don't have one, find a version of the Bible that you can relate to and understand. There are no rules about which Bible to read.

The Holy Spirit, who is your Helper, will help you start to understand God's laws and commandments. Your responses will be different, attitudes changed, and thoughts redirected as well as your actions will be different.

I remember my natural instinct was to be very critical of what people did or said. Once I realized that was not pleasing to God, He opened my ears to what I sounded like and it sounded ugly to me. I asked God to help me correct my reactions. I was amazed to realize, not long after, that I was not offended or critical at things I used to be. I knew I couldn't change myself but that it had to be God that heard my request to make me more like Jesus.

The more we yield ourselves to our Lord to make us a better person, the more we will find that the life in which we once walked no longer appeals to us. We will find more joy and more peace in being obedient to God. We find all His instructions in the Bible are for a reason just because He loves us. There is a purpose behind every one of his laws and statutes. We may not understand right now, but one day, we will.

Our first baptism occurs when we accept Jesus as our Savior and enter His family of believers. Then the Holy Spirit came into our life and literally our bodies to walk with us through the rest of our life to guide us into all truth.

"If you love me, keep my commandments. And I will pray the Father, and He will give you another Helper that He may abide with you forever—the Spirit of truth, whom the world cannot receive because it neither sees Him nor knows Him; but you know Him, for He dwells with you and will be in you." (John 14:15–17)

Jesus Was Baptized by the Holy Spirit

John was the cousin of Jesus and had a special calling from God to be the forerunner of the Messiah. He was to help the people realize they were sinners and needed to repent of their sin. Then, as a symbol of their repentance and a change in their life, John would baptize them or immerse them in water.

Over three years prior to Jesus's ultimate sacrifice on the cross, He left His business, family, and home in Nazareth. On that momentous day, He walked to where His cousin, John, was baptizing people in the Jordan River to be cleansed of their sin. Crowds of people listened to John the Baptist as he taught them and explained God loved them and wanted them to be saved from their sins. Many were convicted of their sin and wanted to be baptized in the river.

We experience water baptism today when we ask Jesus Christ into our lives to symbolize a new beginning, leaving the old life behind and coming up new. Water baptism doesn't save us from our sins, our decision to receive Jesus as our Lord and Savior does. This baptism is an outward sign of an inward decision.

One day, Jesus wove his way through the crowd and asked John to baptize Him. Here was Jesus the Christ, the Son of God who knew no sin, asking John to baptize Him. John knew Jesus as a cousin, but at that moment, he realized that Jesus was the long-awaited Messiah. John, knowing that it was he who should be baptized by Jesus, said he couldn't. John mused, "Why was it that Jesus wanted to be baptized? He didn't need to be cleansed of sin if He was the Son of God!"

However, John finally agreed to baptize Jesus in the river. When he did, a presence came down from heaven and alighted upon Jesus. God then spoke and said, "*You are my beloved Son; in you I am well pleased.*" Now reason with me. If Jesus had no sin and didn't need the baptism of water to be cleansed of sin and He didn't need to be immersed into the family of God because He hadn't yet completed His assignment on earth and that was to die on the cross for the redemption of sin, then what was Jesus being baptized for? "*Then John testified, "I saw the Holy Spirit descending like a dove from heaven and resting upon Him. I didn't know He was the One, but when God sent me to baptize with water, He told me, 'The One on whom you see the Spirit descend and rest is the One who will baptize with the Holy Spirit.'" I saw this happen to Jesus, so I testify that He is the Chosen One of God*" (John 1:32–34).

It wasn't until Jesus had been baptized or immersed by the Holy Spirit that He began His miraculous ministry. Up to that point, Jesus was a carpenter, a citizen of Nazareth and a kind, thoughtful, loving person. But after the baptism of the Holy Spirit, Jesus went into the wilderness for forty days and spent time with God. It was also the time when Jesus was confronted by Satan. It appeared Jesus needed the baptism to have the strength to meet with Satan and develop a bond with the Father.

So it was Jesus who ushered in the baptism of the Holy Spirit for the rest of humanity. This is a different baptism than the infilling of the Holy Spirit. However, humanity wouldn't experience this third baptism until Jesus left the earth and ascended to Heaven. That is why the disciples and others had to go to Jerusalem and wait as Jesus had instructed just before He ascended to heaven.

Jesus, told His disciples, *"Behold, I send the Promise of My Father upon you; but tarry in the city of Jerusalem until you are endued with power from on high"* (Luke 24:49).

The Holy Spirit Gives Power

Jesus had risen from the dead, and for forty days, He was walking and talking to His disciples and many others. He continued to teach about the Kingdom of Heaven reaching many more people who became followers. He wasn't a ghost. He was in human form, but now He had wounds in his hands, feet, and side to show He had been crucified and dead but is now alive.

As his disciples and followers surrounded Him day after day, Jesus was giving instructions to gather in Jerusalem for a very important event. He wanted them to receive the baptism of the Holy Spirit. But why is this baptism necessary? Acts 1:8 Jesus said, *"You will receive power when the Holy Spirit comes upon you. And you will be my witnesses, telling people about me everywhere—in Jerusalem, throughout Judea, in Samaria and to the ends of the earth."*

That word "power" in the Greek means "special miraculous power; the ability to do mighty wonderful works; strength and ability." In other words, those who receive the gift of the baptism of the Holy Spirit will have indwelling within them not only a part of the Godhead; the One that can teach, guide, council, and be with you, but now you can have the ability to do wonderful works through supernatural power to help others. What did Jesus do? He taught about the Kingdom, He laid hands on the sick and they were healed, and cast out demons simply by commanding them. We, too, can have this power if we would believe. Luke, the author of the Gospel of Luke, is also known as the author of the book of Acts. In Acts 1, Luke is giving an account to a friend in this letter. He said, *"The former account I made, O Theophilus, of all that Jesus began both to do and teach, until this day in which He was taken up, after He through the Holy Spirit had given commandments to the apostles whom He had chosen, to whom He also presented Himself alive after His suffering by many infallible proofs being seen by them during forty days and speaking of things pertaining to the kingdom of God"* (Luke 1:1–3).

Jesus was all human, but also all God. That is hard to comprehend, but since He was all God, He was able to defy death, defeat Satan and his plans, and pass power on to all people who would accept these facts. The apostle John explained that Jesus's work on the cross "destroyed the works of the devil" (1 John 3:8b).

Luke continues Jesus's instruction, *"And being assembled together with them, He commanded them not to depart from Jerusalem, but to wait for the Promise of the Father, 'which' He said, 'you have heard from Me: for John truly baptized with water, but you shall be baptized with the Holy Spirit not many days from now"* (Luke 1:4–5).

Here, Jesus needs the disciples to stand by while He finishes the work He came to do in the heavenlies. Understand, the disciples are already filled with the initial infilling of the Holy Spirit because of their belief that Jesus is the Son of God. But Jesus has more for them. The word *baptized* also comes from the Greek, which means to be submerged, saturated, or cover over.

Luke tells us of the supernatural event that took place in that room where there were 120 believers waiting for whatever Jesus had to give them. They might have thought Jesus was going to give them special clothing or a brooch, something that would be special. But instead, the gift Jesus had for them was more special, more powerful than they could have imagined. On that special day, in that room as they were praying, Jesus's followers had total peace and confidence that Jesus would come. There was a sense of expectation that something would happen. Suddenly, the Holy Spirit of the Living God that resided within them came up and over them, saturating them with understanding, boldness, and miracle working power so God would receive all the glory due Him. Those present witnessed what looked like tongues of fire on each person's head. But more amazing, each person started speaking a new language. They were glorifying God as they spoke in unknown tongues. Those on the street heard all the commotion and gathered, listening intently. What was unknown to those in the upper room was that the many dialects they were speaking were understood by the strangers from many nations (Acts 2:1–4). As a result, three thousand people accepted Jesus Christ as their Savior and Lord.

The Holy Spirit Gives the Gift of Tongues

Those in the upper room are not the only ones who received this third baptism. It has continued through the centuries to us today. This gift of what we call "tongues" or "spirit language" is nothing to fear. It is a gift from the throne room of God, and it has many purposes. It isn't very complicated. The spiritual language from God is a language that only God can understand. In 1 Corinthians 14:2, it says, *"For he who speaks in a tongue does not speak to men but to God, for no one understands him; however, in the spirit he speaks mysteries."* The Holy Spirit that resides on the inside of us after the infilling upon our declaration that Jesus is our Lord and Savior comes over and saturates our spirit. This is a way to communicate directly to God through our voice.

Different Ways the Holy Spirit Uses Our Voice

The Holy Spirit knows our heart, our emotions, and what we are going through day to day, minute by minute. When we give our voice over to the Holy Spirit and pray in our spirit language or "tongues," He will pray the perfect prayer on our behalf. Our finite human mind cannot always express our deepest feelings, but the Holy Spirit can. We are giving the Holy Spirit a voice to speak into the atmosphere to make things known and to reveal mysteries. Our spirit-man (the Holy Spirit) is praying the perfect will of God. There is no error in those prayers.

Before you were even born, God had plans and purposes for each one of us. Psalm 139:16 says, *"Your eyes saw my substance being yet unformed. And in Your book they were all written, the days fashioned for me when as yet there were none of them."* As a part of the Godhead, the Holy Spirit knows those plans. When we give our voice over to the Holy Spirit to pray through us, He will pray out our destiny, bringing it into existence. When our voice goes into the atmosphere in our spirit language, we are declaring what God wants for our life.

Also, letting the Holy Spirit use your voice, you are praying for others you may or may not know. You may be praying for a loved one who would be in an accident to be spared. You may be praying for someone's finances to be released at some time in the future. Or you may be praying for a missionary in another land and their protection. Many missionaries have been in extreme danger and cried out to God, while at the same time, the Holy Spirit alerted people on the other side of the world to pray in the Spirit. Those people didn't know who or what they were praying for, but later found that the missionary in danger had been surrounded by angels that only the natives saw and fled sparing the lives of the missionary and his family.

To speak in tongues or your spirit language is immensely powerful, releasing the very heart and desire of God and it is secret. The devil and his demons cannot understand the language. Paul explained, *"He who speaks in a tongue does not speak to men but to God, for no one understands him; however the spirit he speaks mysteries"* (1 Cor. 14:2). There are reasons that God doesn't want Satan to understand this spiritual language. If Satan understood, he could make arrangements to stop the prayer. The person praying is releasing God's will, His protection over His people and releasing prophesies. Also the person is actually edifying himself when no one else can make him feel encouraged. *He who speaks in a tongue edifies himself, but he who prophesies edifies the church* (1 Cor. 14:4). That word *edify* means to instruct or improve yourself. God himself can give you instructions to improve your character, your choices or your attitudes so you can be all that He has determined you can be.

Every person has a different prayer language. What mine sounds like won't sound like yours. This is a gift from God that is just for you. It may start with a quivering lip or one repetitious word or it may be a whole vocabulary. It grows as you become more confident and use it frequently. It can be spoken at any time in conjunction with your natural language. Paul was encouraging those new converts in Thessalonica to pursue what is good for both yourselves and for all. That is to rejoice always and pray without ceasing (1 Thes. 5:16–17). That is pretty hard to do in your natural language, but with your spirit language, you can pray constantly, under your breath at work, at home, on vacation, even in your sleep!

Tongues Used to Speak Prophecy

I will say that sometimes the Holy Spirit will pray through us in a foreign language for the benefit of someone we are with. There are times when someone in a church service from another country needs to hear from God. A message directly for them could turn their life in another direction. There have been times when a foreigner would be sitting in a church service when a message in tongues is given. The message may sound like tongues, but the person hearing the message can hear it in their native tongue. Sound impossible? God is a supernatural God. He does supernatural things all for the benefit for the ones He loves.

Paul again in 1 Corinthians 14:3–5 says, *"But he who prophesies speaks edification and exhortation and comfort to men.*

He who speaks in a tongue edifies himself, but he who prophesies edifies the church. I wish you all spoke with tongues, but even more that you prophesied; for he who prophesies is greater than he who speaks with tongues, unless indeed he interprets, that the church may receive edification."

There are times when a person is led by the Spirit to give a message in tongues in a service, either church or small group. The message is to lift people up, encourage, or give hope. These messages, that are given in an unknown tongue, should be interpreted either by the person giving the message or someone who has the gift of interpretation. Messages are usually instructing, encouraging, or giving direction. This should be done through submitting to the authority in the gathering. It should not be out of order or confusing as God is not the author of confusion.

How to Receive the Gift of the Baptism of the Holy Spirit

When a couple are getting serious about their relationship, thoughts go toward making it permanent—marriage. This is the beginning of making covenant with another person and a gift is given. When the man reaches into his pocket and bends down on a knee, he looks up at his soon-to-be betrothed and extends his hand with a small box in it. As he asks the long-awaited question, he takes the ring out of the box. If this is something she has been looking forward to, she will reach out and take the ring from his hand. She must reach out to receive the token of love. That is what Jesus does with the baptism of the Holy Spirit. He is extending His hand with this gift, His token of love. He loves you so much, He doesn't want you to go through this life without the power and authority He has for you. You have to know about it, want it, look forward to it, and receive His gift. This gift will enable you to break through a whole host of issues you deal with on a daily basis. It is enlightening and liberating.

Imagine on the day the disciples and over one hundred other people were in that upper room waiting for Jesus to reveal the gift He said they would receive. There was great expectation that something special would come. Among the many in that room was Mary, Jesus's mother. The scripture tells us every person that was in the upper room was filled with the Holy Spirit and speaking in unknown tongues. So Mary, the mother of Jesus, also received the gift of a spiritual language.

On that monumental day, Peter, who had denied knowing Jesus when He was on trial, became bold after the baptism of the Holy Spirit. He preached the Good News to everyone and over three thousand people accepted Jesus as their Savior. From that point on, the disciples were more vocal, emboldened, and performed miracles. They did this without Jesus being there in person to encourage them. It was the Holy Spirit that helped and encouraged them.

In John 14:12, Jesus said, *"I tell you the truth, anyone who believes in Me will do the same works I have done, and even greater works, because I am going to be with the Father."* The gift of the baptism of the Holy Spirit is for you and me as believers today. Jesus wants us to help others through miraculous works.

For generations, people have experienced these miraculous powers through this supernatural event. Jesus wants all to hear and experience the power of God. He knew that without the power of tongues, the devil and demons will be able to hear your natural prayers and redirect or stop your petitions. Jesus expects us to pray in tongues. This was not a suggestion. His last directive was those who believe will speak in new tongues: *"And these signs will follow those who believe: In My name they will cast out demons; they will speak with new tongues"* (Matt. 16:17).

You may think, "This is what I've been missing! How do I receive this gift from a supernatural God?" I asked that same question and found that it can happen several ways. First and foremost, you let God know your desire to have this precious gift. It's not a gift that automatically happens. To receive, open yourself up to Him and what I mean by that is make yourself available. If you are not connected with a body of believers who have experienced the baptism of the Holy Spirit, God can still reach you in your home, work, while you're hiking, but the important reality is you are communicating with the Father in heaven.

Many people go to a gathering where there are believers who have experienced the baptism and are willing to help others receive this blessed gift. There may be an explanation of what to expect, then there will be a call to anyone who is willing to receive to come forward as a physical declaration of your faith. There will be people there who will pray or intercede for you because you desire this gift. Then they may gently place their hands on you. No one should force you in any way, but when hands are laid on a person, there is a transference of the Spirit.

The person who is ministering to you, again, is not doing the transferring, but the Holy Spirit is doing it. There may be a feeling that flows through your body, a weakness or shaking. It is natural and in no way is uncomfortable or painful. Imagine the all-powerful Creator God reaching down with His finger and touching you. He is giving you His gift.

Remember the manifestation of speaking in His unknown language? This is where you need to partner with the Holy Spirit and let Him speak through you. But He needs your voice. So as you are receiving, do not try to talk or pray. But let the voice that is bubbling up flow over your vocal chords and through your lips. It may be a stuttering, it may be one word, it may be a whole vocabulary. But whatever comes will sound strange and unrecognizable. Don't stop. That is the Holy Spirit praying through you.

The beautiful thing about speaking in tongues is you can speak whenever the Holy Spirit prompts you. You are the one to release or not release this new language. The more you speak in tongues (which neither you nor anyone else can understand), the more prayers are going up to the throne room of God. On the other hand, you can deny this gift and keep your lips sealed and no heavenly words are going into the atmosphere. I personally opt for praying at all times. You can even pray in your head!

Many times throughout the day, my thoughts settle on the goodness of God, realize how He provides for me, keeps me from harm, or just admiring His handiwork in this world. On those occasions of my praise and worship and my focus on the Lord, the Holy Spirit will rise up and begin to speak. In times of desperation, our spirit language can also cause the Holy Spirit to rise up and manifest in our prayer language. When we don't know how to pray, the Holy Spirit will pray through our spirit.

If you are ready to receive God's perfect gift, pray this out loud:

Heavenly Father, I believe you are the most High God. I believe in Jesus Christ, His birth, death, and resurrection. I now believe You have a gift that you want to give to me and I am ready to receive. Help me know what to do, put me in the path of someone who can help me with questions I have. I want to receive your gift of the Holy Spirit that will endow me with your marvelous power and help me communicate your perfect prayer. In Jesus's name, I pray, Amen.

Chapter 4

Key #3

The Name of Jesus

When we mention a name, we are referring to something or someone. Names are very important to us. They give identity, recognition, and worth. We search diligently for a name that would suit our child. We might name them after a family member, a famous person, or because it is a popular name at the time. We even name our animals, so there is a bond between us and it places value on them.

Names give recognition. Some people are born to a great name, like a king or monarch. They didn't have to do anything but just be born into their family. A great example is the royal family in Great Britain. Queen Elizabeth had a son whom she named Charles. As a person, Charles is a common name, but in the royal household, Charles is "Prince" Charles, the heir to the throne. He was born into a family in which there is instant recognition.

There are some people who have achieved greatness and their names are instantly recognized. Musicians, movie stars, inventors are examples. They may have been born into a normal family, but with talent or intellect, they rose to greatness. For example, Dolly Parton grew up in the hills of Tennessee to a very poor family. She started singing and eventually has become a household name.

Albert Einstein was mentally retarded because he didn't speak until he was four years old. Until he had produced papers and spoke in lectures, Einstein was not widely known. But his intellect won him several Nobel prizes, and thus, he is a well-known name today.

Others with well-known names are considered great because a title was given to them through their accomplishments. For example, Doctor, President, Admiral, Professor, Your Honor, etc. They may have earned the position through their effort with their expectation that they would receive a notable title.

When we think of Jesus of Nazareth, we know he was born into a poor family. A common family. But in the spirit realm, Jesus was born into a royal family and inherited the title as King of kings and Lord of lords. Hebrews 1:2 says, *"Has in these last days spoken to us by His Son whom He has appointed heir of all things, through whom also He made the worlds."* Jesus's name is great because He inherited a great name.

Hebrews goes on in verse 4, saying, *"Having become so much better than the angels, as He has by inheritance obtained a more excellent name than they."* His inheritance didn't come from His natural parents because He had royal blood in His physical body being the son of God.

When the Holy Spirit came on the young virgin Mary, she became pregnant with the Son of God. The blood type of any child will be the same as the father. Mary knew no human intimately when she became pregnant. It was God, the Father, who was the baby Jesus's father. That said, Jesus inherited His

Father's kingdom. Because Jesus Christ was born as royalty, He inherited a great name.

Then, Jesus's name is great because of His achievements. While on earth, He demonstrated great miracles, walked in love toward all people, and ultimately gave up His life so that we can be redeemed from our sins. Philippians 2:5–8 explains how this happened: *"Let this mind be in you which was also in Christ Jesus, who, being in the form of God, did not consider it robbery to be equal with God, but made Himself of no reputation, taking the form of a bond-servant and coming in the likeness of men. And being found in appearance as a man, He humbled Himself and became obedient to the point of death, even the death of the cross. Therefore, God also has highly exalted Him and given Him the name which is above every name, that at the name of Jesus, every knee should bow, of those in heaven, and those on earth, and those under the earth, and that every tongue should confess that Jesus Christ is Lord, to the glory of God the Father."*

Jesus didn't have to leave the beauty and peace of heaven, but for the benefit of all mankind, Jesus stepped out of that incredible place and came to this sin-filled, hateful earth to demonstrate the love of God. When man condemned Him to death by crucifixion, Jesus didn't fight back because this was the will of the Father. Jesus knew He was the only sinless sacrifice that would be able to redeem the sins of man. The result of His selfless act is that we can now commune with the Father God and live with Him for eternity in heaven along with Jesus when our bodies die.

Because of Jesus's work on earth and in death, His name is great because it was conferred upon Him by God. Ephesians 1:20–23 says, *"(God) worked in Christ when He raised Him from the dead and seated Him at His right hand in the heavenly places far above all principality and power and might and dominion, and every name that is named, not only in this age but also in that which is to come. And He put all things under His feet and gave him to be head over all things to the church, which is His body, the fullness of Him who fills all in all."*

Jesus has great position in heaven. He holds all authority over Satan and his demons, authority over man and animals, and He holds authority over the church. I would say that Jesus's name is great! Angels bend their knees in heaven, humans and living beings on earth will bend their knee, and scriptures say that the demons must bow at the name of Jesus. That means submission and honor because His name is the highest name. When Jesus spoke, demons ran, disease left, blind eyes opened, and the lame walked. And that name on our lips will work the same way now as it did then!

Jesus Gives Permission to Use His Name

Jesus told the disciples in John 16:24, *"Until now, you have asked nothing in My name."* You see, as long as Jesus was still alive and talking to his disciples, they didn't have to use His name. But Jesus was handing over the privilege and gave permission to use His name because He knew in a few short days, He wouldn't be with them. We may use the name of Jesus, but we may not realize its significance. We may not realize the authority that comes with it.

We must respect and honor that name and never misuse it! Jesus's name must never be used as a curse or exclamation! His name is meant to be revered and honored.

Jesus gave us the right to use His name, to benefit the Kingdom. We have a right to use that name against our enemy

Satan, to use Jesus's name in our petitions and prayers. We have a right to use His name in our praises and our worship. That name has been given to us to use. It belongs to those in covenant with Him.

When the disciples started ministering after Pentecost, they were like baby birds learning to fly. But with the power of the Holy Spirit that had come upon them, they gained great boldness. They spoke with authority using Jesus's name that resulted in thousands accepting Jesus as their Lord and Savior. They remembered that Jesus told them that *the works He did, they could do and even greater works* (John 14:12). So they started reaching out to heal others.

Jesus had told them before He ascended, *"And whatever you ask in My name, that I will do, that the Father may be glorified in the Son. If you ask anything in My name, I will do it"* (John 14:13, 14).

Let's look at the man at the gate called Beautiful. Jesus and the disciples must have passed by this man dozens of times as they walked to the temple. He was a beggar who had been in that same location for years, lame his whole life. Family members had to deliver him to the gate every day so he could beg for money or food; anything people would give him helped him survive another day.

It was after Jesus had ascended back to heaven that Peter and John were on their way to the temple and approached the gate. This time was different, however. On this day, they focused on him. I can just imagine what was going through their minds! *Can we? Could we? Should we?* So they decided to give this "hard case" a try.

When the lame man saw them, he lifted up his basket and hoped he would get something from these men who were looking at him so intently. Peter said, *"Silver and gold I do not have, but what I do have I give you:* **In the name of Jesus Christ of Nazareth**, *rise up and walk." And he took him by the right hand and lifted him up and immediately his feet and ankle bones received strength"* (Acts 3:1–6) (my emphasis).

Jesus had already declared what would happen when His name was used: *"And these signs will follow those who believe: In My name they WILL cast out demons; they WILL speak with new tongues: they WILL take up serpents (devils) and if they drink anything deadly, it WILL by no means hurt them; they WILL lay hands on the sick and they WILL recover"* (Mark 16:17) (my emphasis).

Jesus didn't give us an option. He didn't say, "If they use My name, they will lay hands on the sick and they might recover." He didn't say, "When you use My name, if I feel like it that day, they will recover." No! There is a definite "will" in each statement. There is no doubt or unbelief there. There is no wondering what Jesus said would happen if we used His name. There is power in the name of Jesus and the devil knows it.

Unfortunately, the devil knows the power in the Name better than most believers. That is why he doesn't want you or me to use the Name. When the name of Jesus is spoken in confidence by a believer who has the revelation of its power, all of Heaven comes to attention. God will listen to prayers that are prayed in Jesus's name. He not only listens to them, He *will* answer them.

Peter and John's use of Jesus's name resulted in the lame beggar walking. A little while later, when everyone was celebrating the miracle in this man, Peter took advantage of the situation to teach. He explained that it was Jesus, whom they (the Pharisees) had crucified when the mob chanted "Crucify Him." He continued, *"You denied the Holy One and the Just, and asked for a murder to be granted to you and killed the Prince of life whom God raised from the dead, of which we are witnesses. And His* name, **through faith in His name**, has made this man strong whom you see and know. Yes, the faith which comes through Him has given him this perfect soundness in the presence of you all" (Acts 3:11–16) (my emphasis).

Seeing Results Using the Name of Jesus

We must always give credit to the Author of life when we see Him work a miracle through us. There is nothing you or I can do ourselves, but with God, all things are possible through Christ Jesus. As a result of this man's healing, more people came into the Kingdom of God by believing that Jesus was truly the Son of the Living God.

Then the religious priests arrived. Peter and John were arrested and taken before the priest's court. They were asked, *"By what power or by what name have you done this?"* Of course Peter and John, filled with the Holy Spirit, shared what happened and said, *"Let it be known to you all and to all the people of Israel, that by the name of Jesus Christ of Nazareth, who you crucified, whom God raised from the dead, by Him this man stands here before you whole"* (Acts 4:7–10).

Some people may ask, "Well, I need to pray and seek God before I lay hands on the sick." OK, pray, but not when you are in front of the sick. You do that in your private time with God. You should have already done your praying. You should have already been to the Father and enjoyed fellowship with Him. We have already talked to Him and asked Him to grant us power over demons so we can help people when that kind of ministry is needed. So when you are talking to a friend, see someone in the grocery store who needs prayer, go and use the power He has granted and exercise the authority given to us through Jesus.

When standing in front of someone who needs healing, there is no need to beg or plead for Jesus to heal. That was accomplished on the cross! It is a time to teach the person needing health and wholeness what the scriptures say. Speak with confidence and boldness and declare that healing come to their body. *"You will also declare a thing, and it will be established for you"* (Job 22:28) and *Call those things which are not as though they are"* (Rom 4:17b). To do anything else is denying Jesus to do the work for which He died on the cross. It is for you to use His name with power and authority.

I would like to tell you my experiences in using the Name of Jesus. I took the Word literally when it said that at the name of Jesus every knee will bow. When I thought about it, animals have knees. So when a snarling, growling dog approached me one day, I said, "In the name of Jesus, I command you to leave!" The dog looked at me, stopped growling, and went to lie on the porch of the house in total peace.

While driving at the speed posted, I sometimes get an aggressive driver that gets way too close to my back bumper. I watch for a while to see if they will change their behavior. When it goes on too long, I will declare, "In the Name of Jesus, back off!" Every time, and I mean every time, they lift their foot off the gas pedal and they back off.

Those are just everyday occurrences in which you can see the power of the name of Jesus at work. It is not frivolous when you know for a fact that you have authority over living things on this earth. Simple things, but now let's look at the more important work the name of Jesus does.

The name of Jesus causes results to happen. I was at a crusade in Honduras where the pastor had finished his message and told us to pray with the people. I don't speak Spanish. The woman I was praying for didn't speak English. So I used my spiritual language that neither one of us understood, but I was praying in the name of Jesus. She had just received Jesus as her Savior that night. I had no idea this woman had any health issues. As I was praying in tongues, in my mind, I prayed that she would be whole from the top of her head to the bottom of her feet.

After I had returned from that trip, I was in my office and got a phone call from our missionary friend who heard from that lady's pastor in Honduras. Apparently, the woman I had prayed for had terminal cancer, so as soon as she could, she went to her doctor and told him she had been healed. He tested her and confirmed she had been healed. But how did she know to go to the doctor? Because although I was praying in my spirit language, she heard me praying in Spanish! She understood everything I said. The Lord had spoken to her through my prayer, saying she was healed. Her obedience in going to the doctor confirmed God's word.

That is what glorifies the Father. To do something that will advance the Kingdom here on earth. Can you imagine when she praised her new Savior and told everyone she could about her miraculous healing, they listened? That is what pulls people toward Jesus.

Demons must also bend their knee to the Name of Jesus. When Jesus spoke, demons ran, disease left, blind eyes opened, and the lame walked. That same name on our lips will work the same way now, as it did then! Nothing has passed away. *Jesus Christ is the same yesterday, today, and forever* (Hebrews 13:8).

When we get it in our spirits that we are heirs of God and joint heirs of Jesus Christ, we realize the power Jesus had also resides in us. Romans 8:16–17 says, *"The Spirit Himself bears witness with our spirit that we are children of God, and if children, then heirs— heirs of God and joint heirs with Christ, if indeed we suffer with Him that we may also be glorified together."* I believe that when you know who you are in Christ, through the covenant you have with God, with the baptism of the Holy Spirit and using the name of Jesus, you *will* see miracles.

Another example I can share the power of the name of Jesus is through weather. I know that strong believers had tornadoes come directly toward their home and, using the name of Jesus, commanded the winds and the rain to change course and it did. In one case I heard, the large tornado split in two, going around the home or neighborhood, then came back together on the other side.

I have also spoken to the weather. I was at a crusade in Nigeria, Africa, and that particular night was assigned to run camera that was on a tall platform in the middle of the crowd of tens of thousands. From my vantage point, over in the distance behind the stage, I saw very dark clouds moving toward the crusade field with lightning jumping in and out of the clouds. I knew that a storm would disperse the crowd and all equipment would have to be protected and the evening would be ruined. I knew who was behind this storm, and I got angry at the devil! They needed to hear the message that could change their lives! So with all the authority I knew I had, I spoke to the storm to cease and leave the area. The next time I looked up at the sky, it was clear! I give all praise to God who can defeat the plans of the enemy, Satan.

I was on a small boat going to a church to ordain a pastor of a tiny church on the banks of the Amazon River in Peru. There were several of us traveling, four or five from the Peruvian home church, my husband Bob, and our missionary host. As we were boarding this small craft, I looked down the river in the direction we were headed and saw dark clouds ahead. I didn't realize at that time, but the trip was to take about an hour and a half. Sure enough, we ran into rain. Not a gentle rain but a blowing rain that caused white caps on this huge river. Even with curtains down on the sides, we were getting soaked!

I started to think about what my appearance would be, hair soaked, as well as our clothes and I got angry. I thought, *This cannot be good to show up soaked! I am to be the ambassador of our Most High God!* Immediately I heard in my inner being, "Jesus spoke to the wind and the rain!" I thought about it a minute and remembered the name of Jesus had the power I needed, so under my breath, I said, "In the name of Jesus of Nazareth, wind and rain, stop!" I declared something that didn't look like could possibly happen, but within one or two minutes, the rain stopped, the wind stopped, and the sun came out!

I was in India with another team. The pastor had finished preaching and sent all of the team out to minister to the sick. I am surrounded by hundreds of precious Indians reaching out to me with their hands for me to touch, to bless, to love on them. I felt like an octopus with eight arms, trying to minister to as many people as I could all the while praying in the Holy Spirit.

Suddenly, a very old woman was beside me that was bent over at the waist. The pastor who brought the message that night gave a beautiful illustrated sermon on the woman who was bent over for eighteen years. When I saw this old Indian woman, I broke into tears and said to the Lord, "If no one else gets healed tonight, let it be this one." I laid my hands on her and said, "In the name of Jesus of Nazareth, be made whole!" I placed my right hand on the small of her back and my left hand on her chest, then applied gentle pressure to both areas. She started to straighten up until she was totally upright. The beautiful smile on her face glowed, and she started jumping up and down! Everyone around rejoiced and all I could say was, "Thank you, Jesus!" I knew it was not my power, but the power in the covenant, the Holy Spirit working through me and the name of Jesus. I simply was there at the right time, in the right atmosphere and confident that Jesus heals.

As a believer, we have every right to use the name of Jesus that He transferred to us through His sacrifice on the cross. To not use it when the appropriate opportunity arrives is to deny Jesus to receive the glory and honor He deserves.

Chapter 5

Key #4

Authority of the Believer

Jesus lived His life on the earth doing what God the Father wanted Him to do. His assignment was to show love and compassion to a world that was overwhelmed with sickness, greed, lust, hate, jealousy, envy, pride, and on and on. Jesus walked from village to village in Galilee talking about the kingdom of heaven and the blessings that will come as a result of being a part of it. He healed the sick, commanded the demons to obey, showed compassion, and loved everyone He met.

On the surface, He looked like any other man. He didn't glow or have a mystical halo over his head. He looked like every other Jew in Israel. Like any other human, he was flesh and blood and knew that He would not be on the earth forever. But Jesus was very different. He was all man, but also all God, living a perfect and sinless life. He taught His closest friends all about the Kingdom and the future, knowing all along that His life on this earth would soon be over. His enemies from the religious sect felt Jesus was a threat to their carefully preserved laws. They reasoned, if Jesus were to persuade too many people to believe that He was the Son of God, then the designated religious leaders would lose their power over the people. Not only that, but the Romans would look at this religious sect as unnecessary and intervene in their religious practices.

To get the Romans involved, the Pharisees and Sadducees started making up lies about Jesus and accused Him of heresy and that Jesus pronounced that He was a king. Eventually, their plan worked and Jesus was accused of a crime punishable by crucifixion and died a horrible death—the most violent way to die through the torture of hanging on a cross until you suffocated.

After his friends had buried Jesus in a borrowed tomb, the disciples thought (as we would have thought) that it was over! They had dedicated three years of their lives to this man, and now it has come to this! He was put in the grave, and now they are asking what will they do with their lives?

However, while they were looking at their personal situation and pondering their future, Jesus was working on our behalf. Again, I say, Jesus was all human so when His heart stopped, He died a physical death. However, Jesus was also all God and left heaven for the purpose He was about to accomplish. While the disciples were grieving and while the body of Jesus was in the tomb, the Spirit of Jesus left the tomb and went to hell where Satan and his demons live.

Jesus was to do something no other human could do. That was to be the ultimate sinless sacrifice in order to redeem mankind back to God. Up to that time, there were only symbolic animal sacrifices made at the temple to appease the Creator of the Universe because of our inherent sinful nature. Now, through the sacrifice of Jesus, the Son of God, He became the only One who could stand in the gap between God and man. He had no sin. Philippians 2:5–8 reads: *"Let this mind be in you which was also in Christ Jesus, who, being in the form of God, did not consider it robbery to be equal with God, but made Himself of no reputation, taking on the form of a bond-servant and coming in the likeness of men. And being found in appearance of a man, He humbled Himself and became obedient to the point of death, even the death of the cross."* Therefore, Jesus did what no human could have done and that was to defeat sin and death through His death on the cross.

Adam and Eve Transferred Their Authority to Satan

In the book of Genesis is the account of Adam and Eve disobeying God by eating from a specific tree. In Gen. 2:16–17, God spoke to Adam, saying, *"Of every tree of the garden you may freely eat; but of the tree of the knowledge of good and evil you shall not eat, for in the day that you eat of it you shall surely die."* Adam told Eve about that specific tree. One day, she was looking for her next meal, and the following conversation between her and a serpent (Satan) occurred (Gen. 3:2–5). *The woman said to the serpent "We may eat the fruit of the trees of the garden but of the fruit of the tree which is in the midst of the garden, God has said, 'You shall not eat it, nor shall you touch it, lest you die.'" Then the serpent said to the woman, "You will not surely die. For God knows that in the day you eat of it your eyes will be opened and you will be like God, knowing good and evil."*

So Eve, being deceived by Satan, took the fruit, disobeying her Lord. By doing that, all of mankind automatically became sinful. Adam and Eve became the first to rebel and disobey God and became sinners. At that very moment, they had lost any authority they had on the earth, and it was transferred to the great deceiver, Satan.

Since Satan is the one who legally received authority from Adam, he has perpetuated man's sinful rebellion, pride, greed, and lustful characteristics in mankind. There is only One who could conquer those efforts, and that is the Son of God, Christ Jesus. *"And you, being dead in your trespasses and the uncircumcision of your flesh, He has made alive together with him, having forgiven you all sins, having wiped out the handwriting of requirements that was against us, taken it out of the way, having nailed it to the cross. Having disarmed principalities and powers, He made a public spectacle of them, triumphing over them in it"* (Col. 2:13–15).

It is Jesus who had to go to hell and take back the keys of authority and power that Satan had held since the original sin in the Garden of Eden. Although Satan was delighted with the fact that Jesus was dead, perhaps he hadn't thought that Jesus would actually confront him in his home court!

Imagine his surprise when Jesus appeared and commanded Satan to return the keys of power and authority that he had held since Adam released them to him. This was one of the main reasons Jesus had to return to the earth. He had to give His perfect sinless human life in order to make it possible for you and me to have a personal relationship with God AND to be able to have the same power and authority that Jesus held when He walked the earth. Jesus re-introduced the Kingdom of God which was lost in the Garden of Eden back to mankind. By obeying God and completing His task, Jesus enabled mankind to regain what was lost to Satan in the Garden of Eden: our authority through the declaration of God.

Jesus Transfers Authority to Mankind

Several months earlier, Jesus was meeting with His disciples that momentous day when He asked them, *"Who do men say that I am?"* When Simon Peter confessed that Jesus was the Christ, the Son of the living God, Jesus proclaimed, *"Blessed are you, Simon Bar-Jonah for flesh and blood has not revealed this to you, but My Father who is in heaven. And I also say to you that you are Peter and on this rock I will build My church and the gates of Hades shall not prevail against it. And I will give you the keys of the kingdom of heaven and whatever you bind on earth, will be bound in heaven and whatever you loose on earth will be loosed in heaven"* (Matt. 16:17–19).

Never again would Satan have legal power and authority over those who believe in Jesus as long as they know who they are as a Christian. By that I mean, one who has asked Jesus to be their Lord and Savior and know for certain they are a child of the King, not only in their head, but in their heart, will speak with conviction. Believers have been given the keys of the Kingdom of Heaven. It is up to us to use them in an effective way.

The disciples weren't aware of the confrontation in hell, but they were about to experience the greatest and most thrilling life beyond their imagination. After only three days in the grave, an angel of God moved the stone that had been rolled in front of the tomb, sealing it so no one could get in or get out. To display an empty grave was to show Jesus's followers that His body was gone and had risen from the dead, just as He had described. At first, they were alarmed because they didn't remember all that Jesus had told them was going to happen. He had tried to prepare them that He not only was going to die, but that He was going to live again. But with all the trauma they had experienced, they had forgotten.

Jesus appeared to the disciples several times after His resurrection over the course of many weeks to continue to teach and explain all that he taught before the cross and confirming His resurrection. Then it came time for Him to leave and return to the Father in Heaven. But before He left humanity to be on their own on this earth, He had to transfer His **Authority** so that you and I would have Key #4 of the Kingdom of Heaven.

Jesus told them before He went to the cross what was to happen. *"I still have many things to say to you, but you cannot bear them now. However, when He, the Spirit of truth has come, He will guide you into all truth, for He will not speak on His own authority, but whatever He hears He will speak; and He will tell you things to come. He will glorify Me, for He will take of what is Mine and **declare** it to you. All things that the Father has are Mine. Therefore, I said that He will take of Mine and declare it to you"* (John 16:12–15) (my emphasis). That word *declare* means "to report, speak, or show something from heaven to those who are Kingdom people." Jesus transferred what He brought from heaven to His church to use as a tool or weapon against the powers of hell.

Using Our Authority

Peter, the representative of the Church (Matt. 16:18), received the same authority that Jesus operated in. That authority is over all plans and strategies the devil has set against you, your family, and all of humankind. Again, Peter is the representative of the Church. The Church has never ceased. The church is all denominations that believe in the birth, death and resurrection of Jesus Christ. This means if you are part of the Church, by being a part of the Kingdom of God on this side of heaven, you and I have the same authority on earth that Jesus did!

"The Spirit Himself bears witness with our spirit that we are the children of God, and if children, then heirs—heirs of God and joint heirs with Christ" (Romans 8:16–17a). Again, Jesus said to Peter, who is the representative of the Church and we are now the Church, *"Whatever you bind on earth, will be bound in heaven and whatever you loose on earth will be loosed in heaven"* (Matt 16:19). So I have to ask, what is keeping us from binding Satan's work and loosening the power of heaven?

The apostle John wrote, *"He who sins is of the devil, for the devil has sinned from the beginning. For this purpose, the Son of God was manifested, that He might destroy the works of the devil"* (1 John 3:8). Although Satan has been defeated in his works through our authority doesn't mean he isn't still putting false thoughts in our heads. He still works us into a frenzy of fear making us to feel we have to have no authority over what he does in our lives. He can make us feel that we are defeated and there is no hope! All of that is a lie! Satan is still around to do his dirty work, but we have been given the ability to cast those thoughts down (2 Cor. 10:3–5), and declare who we are in Christ. Once we get hold of the truth that we have authority over Satan, he will be defeated in our lives.

Our feelings will come and they will go. One day, we may feel we can conquer these feelings like a giant, then the next, we will feel hopeless and defeated. We cannot let the enemy push us around like that. Knowing who we are in Jesus Christ, that we are a joint heir and have the same authority He carried, should level out those feelings.

After walking with the disciples and many others for forty days after His physical death and resurrection, Jesus knew it was time for Him to leave. So with great emotion and passion, Jesus said, *"ALL authority has been given to Me in heaven and on earth. Go, therefore and make disciples of all the nations, baptizing them in the name of the Father, and of the Son and of the Holy Spirit, teaching them to observe all things that I have commanded you, and lo, I am with you always, even to the end of the age"* (Matt 28:18–20).

In the spirit realm, Jesus's words delivered *all authority* to us. The word **authority** means jurisdiction, power, the right, and delegated influence. Through those words Jesus spoke to His disciples, He delegated all the authority to the Church and gives us back the legal authority Adam and Eve held. Now Satan has *no* legal right to hold the tiniest amount of authority over us!

What do we do with that authority? Well, we have been authorized to overthrow the works of the devil, God's number one enemy! Jesus came to destroy the *works* of the devil and now we have been authorized to do the same!

We have been authorized to heal the sick.

We have been authorized to cast out demons.

We have been commanded and authorized to GO and preach the gospel (good news) of the Kingdom.

This is what Jesus did during His life and He has declared into the atmosphere that He wants us to continue what He started. Jesus was only one man, but when He authorized the Church (that's us), He just multiplied Himself by the millions. We aren't supposed to be just churchgoers—that's what Satan wants. Jesus expects us to go into the world! That's your home, neighborhood, workplace, and even other countries. We aren't supposed to wait until we get to heaven because we won't need that authority in heaven! It is on earth and in our lives today that the devil is roaming around seeking whom he will devour

(1 Peter 8). Remember, we have been crowned as heirs of God and joint heirs with Jesus Christ. Sounds like we have authority to me, how about you?

To give a word picture of how we are to look in the spirit realm: I'm sure you have seen a policeman or woman standing in the street directing traffic at one time or another. How is he dressed? He has on a uniform and a badge to indicate he has a position. But it's when he/she puts up their hand in order to stop the one-ton car that shows the authority they carry. The power of that uniformed person can control big heavy cars and trucks with a one hand signal and they stop. That is how we are to look in the spirit realm. We hold up our hands and tell the devil to *stop* his maneuvers against our bodies, family, finances, friends, job place, etc.

The apostle Peter had been cowardly and lacked confidence and power before his experience with the baptism of the Holy Spirit. Now, let's look again at Peter and John after Pentecost. They approach the lame man at the Gate Beautiful. They knew he had been there a long time because they had passed by him for years. Now, they look at him through different eyes. They have tremendous compassion on him and know they can help him if he would believe they could. Peter and John knew the man is looking for a handout, but Peter said something that surprised the invalid. He said, "I don't have any money, but this is what I do have...*in the name of Jesus Christ of Nazareth*, rise up and walk."

Now, that is what I call "speaking with authority." Not only did they command him to rise up, they gave him a lending hand and lifted him up. What happened then? His feet and ankle bones received strength! Peter and John were speaking in that power and authority that Jesus passed on to them.

To bring an illustration into our homes, when you have a child who is being unruly or disobedient, the best way to get their attention is to use a different voice. You exert your authority by the tone of your voice to get their attention. That is how you must exert your authority with the devil. As believers, we have gained entrance through Jesus Christ into the Kingdom of God. As a result, we have been given authority to exert our power over the dominion of the devil in our lives.

Jesus gave the disciples and the Church the authority to use the name of Jesus. But would it do any good to just "think" His name? Would it do any good just to "think" about the authority we hold? No! Does a traffic police officer stand in the middle of the intersection and just "think" about the power he holds over those cars? No! He has his uniform and badge in which he is dressed, but he also uses his hands and he may have white gloves and a whistle. He has to use those tools as well as being cloaked in the uniform and badge.

Authority and power is not just thinking and knowing, but it is action. Jesus has given us all authority and he expects us to exert that authority. We must move beyond knowing and step into action, which is called Faith.

Jesus said, *"Have faith in God. For assuredly I say to you, whoever says to this mountain, 'Be removed and be cast into the sea,' and does not doubt in his heart but believes that those things he says will be done, he will have whatever he says. Therefore, I say to you, whatever things you ask when you pray, believe that you receive them and you will have them"* (Mark 11:23–24).

Jesus said, we must speak to our circumstances. That could be cancer, sugar diabetes, your finances, family drama, and many other obstacles we face. We must speak without doubt or unbelief. We cannot doubt our abilities, doubt God, doubt the

Word, or doubt our authority. Look what Jesus says will happen when we believe and speak! *You will have whatever things you ask when you pray with authority.*

At this point in this book, you will understand that with the covenant you hold with the Creator of the Universe, your Father, you are in protective care and God has your back. As long as you have His back, He will have all of heaven at attention over you. You also have One who is by your side, the Holy Spirit. He is there to teach, comfort, guide, and tell you of things you couldn't make up or read. He will always be by your side: in good times and in bad. There is also the weapon of the name of Jesus. He gave His life so you could use His name. Jesus expects you to use His name when you are in warfare with the devil, when you are petitioning for others, when you are seeking wisdom and so on. With God the Father and Jesus and the Holy Spirit on your side, you have all the power and authority to defeat the enemy.

Chapter 6

Key #5

Commanding Power

With the understanding that you have read thus far in the book, it should come naturally that you begin to use authoritative power which is in the tone and force of your voice over your circumstances.

Let's begin with how Jesus handled a situation. There's a story in Mark 9:14. It begins with a father whose son has seizures that throw him into fire and water. This is not normal. It is caused by demonic activity and the father knows it. So he goes to the disciples while Jesus is away praying. The disciples had seen Jesus do many strange and wonderful things. They also knew that Jesus had given them power over the devil, but being so new to this concept, they attempted to cast out and heal the boy, but to no avail.

A little later, Jesus arrives, and the father approaches Him to explain the situation. He said, "I spoke to Your disciples, that they should cast it out, but they could not." I'm sure Jesus looked at His disciples with disappointment on His face. He chastised them about their lack of faith, then asked the father to bring the boy to Him.

Once the boy was in the presence of Jesus, he immediately started convulsing, fell on the ground, and wallowed, foaming at the mouth. Jesus knew the devil was very aware He was there. Although He already knew the answer Jesus asked the father, "How long has this been happening to him?"

The father said, "From childhood. And often, he has thrown the child both into the fire and into the water to destroy him. But if You can do anything, have compassion on us and help us."

Jesus replied, "If you can believe, all things are possible to him who believes."

Immediately, the father of the boy cried out and said with tears, "Lord, I believe; help my unbelief!"

A crowd was beginning to gather by this time. But here is what is important. Jesus rebuked that unclean spirit, saying to it in a commanding voice, "Deaf and dumb spirit, I command you, come out of him and enter him no more!" (Mark 9:25).

The result? The spirit screamed through the boy, convulsed him greatly, and came out of him. The child looked like he was dead, but Jesus reached down and took him by the hand and lifted him up (Mark 9:14–27).

What Is a Commanding Voice?

There are many things to mention here, but the most important was how Jesus handled the devil. He didn't ask politely, He didn't pray, Jesus spoke with that commanding voice, knowing He had power and demanded the demonic spirits to leave the boy. They had no choice but to obey.

When we, as Christians, know that all authority has been given to us from Jesus, that we are heirs of God and joint heirs of Jesus Christ, then we, too, can handle similar situations with the same results.

Many times, I have witnessed people crying and pleading that Jesus do something in a certain situation. That is totally unnecessary. Jesus cried out on the cross, "It is finished." That meant that Jesus had completed everything He was sent to do. He was to save, deliver, and restore mankind back to God. With that one event, all future generations were given the Kingdom that Satan had stolen centuries before from Adam and Eve. He handed to us the keys of the Kingdom to yield our power over sin and sickness. He has taken a seat at the right hand of God the Father. Now everything dealing with life is in our hands and our mouth. *Death and life are in the power of the tongue and those who love it will eat of its fruit* (Prov. 18:21).

Jesus was very committed to revealing to the disciples the importance of using their voice to command results. He was walking with them one day and saw a fig tree that was in full leaf. He went to see if He could find something to eat, but when they arrived, they saw there was nothing but leaves, for it was not the season for figs. Jesus's response was, "*Let no one eat fruit from you ever again.*" The disciples heard what He had said (Mark 11:12–14).

Don't you think that the Creator of the Universe knew that it was not fig season? Do you think that Jesus expected to find figs in the tree? No, Jesus knew exactly what He was doing, and that was to teach the disciples how to command and get results.

The next morning, Jesus and the disciples passed by the same fig tree and saw that it had dried up from the roots. Peter, remembering what Jesus spoke over the tree, said to Jesus, "Rabbi, look! The fig tree which You cursed has withered away."

Jesus stopped walking and turned to His small group. He said, *"Have faith in God. For assuredly, I say to you, whoever says to this mountain, 'Be removed and be cast into the sea, and does not doubt in his heart but believes that those things he says will be done, he will have whatever he says. Therefore, I say to you, whatever things you ask when you pray, believe that you receive, and you will have them"* (Mark 11:23–24).

It is my opinion that Jesus intentionally demonstrated the commanding power of His words when He cursed the fig tree. He wanted the disciples to watch and learn the power of authority where there was no doubt and make it a teaching moment. How many of us can say that they speak to impossible situations with no doubt in our heart? Do we expect God to hear and answer our petitions when we are doubtful? Jesus restored the Kingdom of Heaven back to the earth. Our confidence must be in what Jesus accomplished through His death, regaining of the keys of the Kingdom and destroying the works of the devil. Through our understanding and confidence, we will see miracles again.

There are many, many examples of that kind of belief. A belief where a change in circumstances is expected and anticipated. The apostle Peter was a firm believer of commanding power. There would be an impossible situation in the natural, but with a firm and controlled voice, he demanded a change in a person's life. For example, he was traveling and found a man named Aeneas who had been bedridden eight years because of paralysis. So Peter said to him, "Aeneas, Jesus the Christ heals you. Arise and make your bed." Then, miraculously, he rose out of that bed immediately (Acts 9:32–34).

The Apostle Peter had found a group of women in Joppa who were very interested in hearing about Jesus. One of the women was named Dorcas who became committed to Christ and helped many people. One day, she became very ill and died. While her body was being prepared for burial, two disciples ran to Peter and asked him to come quickly. Peter was taken to the room where Dorcas lay. He asked all those who were mourning her to leave. He prayed, then spoke in a commanding voice to Dorcas, saying, "Tabitha (Daughter), arise." She opened her eyes, and when she saw Peter, she sat up. He helped her stand and then called in her friends, showing them Dorcas was alive (Acts 9:36–42).

The Apostle Paul also knew of the commanding power and his authority over situations the devil brought upon people. As Paul was on his way to a prayer meeting, a slave girl possessed with a spirit of divination followed him and his friends. She was crying out, saying, "These men are the servants of the Most High God, who proclaim to us the way of salvation." She did this day after day. The scriptures don't say this, but I imagine her tone or attitude was not reverent or in awe but more mocking. After many days of this, Paul was greatly annoyed, turned, and said to the spirit, "I command you in the name of Jesus Christ to come out of her." And that spirit came out that very hour (Acts 16:16–18).

Whether be sickness, infirmity, or the torments of the devil, all must obey when a child of the Most High God knows their authority. When a believer uses the name of Jesus with confidence, the results are healing, wholeness, or the devil leaves. We have been given that right and are expected to use our authority.

Learning to Use Our Voice of Authority

Many years ago, as one who had just recently received the baptism of the Holy Spirit, I had several anointed pastors as mentors. Through their encouragement, I started to exert my authority over what I thought were impossible circumstances. People who would otherwise have been dealing with physical situations for the rest of their lives were healed. Not because of me or my abilities, but because I made myself available to be used by the Lord.

We were on a mission trip in Ukraine where I was part of a team. One Sunday, we were split into several smaller teams to visit churches in the city we were ministering in. The pastor of the team I was with preached his sermon, then we were sent to pray for the people. There was a woman whose joints in her hands were swollen, and her fingers were drawn up into the palms of her hands. She was fairly young and a mother of several children. I knew she had to have the use of her hands, but with arthritis, she was unable to do the simplest tasks without extreme pain.

In tears, she told me she wanted Jesus to heal her. I understood I was the vessel sent to help her. I cannot heal. Jesus heals through me because I know I am in covenant with God. I carry all the power Jesus did, and with the authority, He delivered to me. I began to teach her about how much God loved her and that He wanted her healed. Without any reservation, I commanded that the arthritis and inflammation leave her body. I spoke health to her, that she be whole from the top of her head to the bottom of her feet, in the name of Jesus of Nazareth.

After praying for her and commanding her body to respond, I said, "Let's see what God did. Open your hands."

She looked at me with the most surprised face as she pulled her fingers out straight. She made a fist and, again, spread her fingers out straight. Then she started rejoicing and so did everyone around her.

Besides my own experiences, there are some profound miracles that I personally have witnessed on the mission field. We were a mission team in Ebaguay, Colombia, South America, where my son, Jason, was part of the team. We were new to the baptism of the Holy Spirit and the miracles He performed through us. It's amazing to me that with just a small amount of faith, but an act of obedience that God works through us.

We were ministering in a park where there were many Colombians milling around. Our pastor had preached a message, then sent us, the team, to pray for people. A young man came up to Jason to be healed. He showed Jason an ugly rash on both his arms and asked Jason to pray for him.

As a young, newly baptized in the Holy Spirit believer, Jason was tentative, but bold as well. After talking to this young man, he prayed and commanded that the young man be healed, in the Name of Jesus. Jason's experience in healing was new, but he knew it was through his faith that God was able to heal this young man.

After the prayer was over, the young man looked at his arms, expecting them to be clear of the rash. Jason said, "Don't worry, God will heal you," and went about praying for others.

A little later, the young man came back, looked at his arms, then at Jason and said, "I'm not healed yet! Jason said, "I know God will heal you. Be patient."

The guy walked away again but looked discouraged.

That night, our large team was split into two groups to be housed in two different locations. Jason's group was taken to a church where the morning's service was to be held. They slept on mattresses on the floor of the sanctuary. Early the next morning, as they were preparing for the morning services, Jason turned and saw that same young man heading toward the church.

Jason turned his back to the door and whispered up a prayer. "Lord, what am I to do if he isn't healed?" The young man burst through the door and walked right up to Jason, showing his arms to him.

"Look," he said, "I'm healed."

Jason witnessed that the arms that had been covered with a rash was as clear as a baby's skin. God did heal, just not immediately.

We are never to think we do the healing. When God heals, it is in His timing. I believe through Jason's faith and the young man's expectation, God was able to heal.

I can't stop sharing these miracles because God wants you to know He is still the Healer. He is the same yesterday, today, and forever!

Many times, I have commanded pain in my own body to leave, and it did within seconds. Yes, you can speak over your own body! There were medical situations that looked like it wanted to settle in my body for the rest of my life. My mother and sisters suffer with annoying foot pain. My feet started to have a lot of problems, including bunions. One day, I decided that I had had enough! I knew that Jesus had taken all my pain and all my sickness and torment on the cross and that I didn't need to bear this pain.

So I prayed something like this: Lord, I am too young to deal with this affliction for the rest of my life. It hinders my ability to work for you, and I won't receive this disease. So with the authority you have given me, I say, "In the name of Jesus, I command the enemy to cease and desist all maneuvers against me. No weapon formed against me will prosper! I command the inflammation to leave, pain to go, and my body to be strong and healthy from the top of my head to the bottom of my feet." Immediately, the familiar pain left my foot. Whenever the pain tries to return, I command it to go!

When I started speaking over other people, they were relieved of disease and discomfort, from toothaches to cancers. In the coming days, months, and years, our faith is going to be challenged. We must be totally convinced that what Jesus did for us on the cross was done not only to redeem us and reserve a space for us in heaven, but to give us a life of victory here and *now*.

In order to make it through the coming hostility against Christians, we must be completely confident in these Keys of the Kingdom. I challenge you to read the gospels with new eyes as Jesus shares about the Kingdom of God and see if you will look at your life in a totally different way. Then use your voice to praise God, pray in your spirit language out loud, as you pray, finish your prayers "in the Name of Jesus," and begin to use your authority by commanding situations to change.

Our responsibility as ambassadors of the Kingdom of God on this earth today is to share the Kingdom. Jesus went about all the cities and villages, saying, "The Kingdom of God is *near*." He could say that because He brought it to the earth. But it wasn't consummated until his death on the cross. We can now say, "The kingdom of God is *here,* and it is for you."

Jesus said, "I am the way, the truth and the life, no one comes to the Father but through me" (John 14:6). Jesus is the door, the only way to step into the kingdom. Once someone believes on Jesus, His life, death, burial, and resurrection, and believes in their heart, then they are saved from their sin and separation from God. But we are still living on this side of heaven and that is why Jesus gave us back the dominion that Adam lost in the Garden of Eden. It is for us to use *now*. Jesus gave the keys to Peter who represented the Church. Now you, as a believer, have the keys of the kingdom! You are to use them to open the doors to preach to the lost and minister to the sick and tormented.

The fact that Jesus commanded us to go into all the world and make disciples gives us every right to exert our authority with demonstrations of power that result in the miraculous. Step out of your comfort zone and be the ambassador of God that will result in new boldness and power.

Chapter 7

Binding and Loosing

Matthew 16:19 says, *"And I will give you the keys of the kingdom of heaven and whatever you bind on earth will be bound in heaven, and whatever you loose on earth will be loosed in heaven."*

In Matthew 16:19 Jesus knew what He was saying to His disciples. I will paraphrase; "When you use the keys that I have handed over to you, you will have the authority to make a difference in the lives of people who are under the influence of Satan." As the legal heir of Jesus Christ, you are the hands and feet that all of heaven needs in order to be a world changer.

What Does It Mean to Bind?

Now, let me explain what Jesus was talking about when He said, "Whatever you bind on earth will be bound in heaven." The word *bind* or *bound* means there is a situation where one is hampered, constrained, or prevented from free movement or action. We meet people in that situation all the time. It may be addictions like drugs, alcohol, food, pornography, sex, exercise, TV, gambling, and on and on. These people are bound by an element in their lives that keeps them from living a life of freedom because their addiction is all they think about. It is their god.

Addiction is a trap of the enemy, Satan. He wants people bound up, so they won't focus on God or His plans and purposes for their lives. They become consumed with the thought and action that seems satisfying for the moment, but in reality, it is a great trap to keep them from a life of freedom, joy, and peace.

Perhaps you have a loved one who has terminal or chronic illness and is scared of the future. Teach them about a loving Savior who cares about them and wants them to live. Then let them know Jesus is the Healer, and if they want to be healed, He will do it. Teaching is the principle element to getting someone saved and healed. I will probably shock some, but a person doesn't need to be saved before Jesus will heal them. Sometimes, a miraculous healing will get them to believe. My pastor used to say, "Healing is the dinner bell for salvation." Get them healed, then they will listen to the salvation message. It's not necessary to go in a particular order.

We can be bound by sickness and disease. I know of people who are so bound by medicine they think that is the only thing that can help. Unfortunately, many people go to the doctor first before going to the great Physician for answers. Remember, the Holy Spirit is to guide and counsel you. He can tell you what the problem is and give insight on how to deal with it.

I had an experience where I had acid reflux or GERD. I dealt with it by taking antacids until I felt I needed to go to the doctor. Tests were done several times where the doctor saw a lot of inflammation and prescribed something stronger.

I didn't like taking any pharmaceuticals, so that's when I asked the Holy Spirit to help me identify why this was so persistent. One day, out of the blue, I heard in my head the voice of the Holy Spirit. He told me I was taking my vitamins right before bed, and they didn't have a chance to get all the way down into my stomach before I laid down. They were dissolving in my esophagus! Oh, I felt so foolish! All the doctor's visits, all the medicine, and all I had to do was take the vitamins earlier in the day. When I changed my timetable, it was within days that there was a noticeable change. No more inflammation, no more acid reflux.

We can also be bound in our minds. Our thinking can be so distorted that we get frozen. The primary weapon of Satan is fear. If he can get you to be afraid, then he's got you bound. The worst bondage is when there is a phobia. That is when someone is so frozen with fear they cannot get beyond that fear to live a normal life. It takes a lot of determination to defeat a fear of that extreme, but with the help of God's truth and knowing God's got your back, one can defeat the spirit of fear.

In the Old Testament is the famous story of a young shepherd who had brothers in the Israelite army. David was sent to take food to his brothers, but instead saw the army faced an enemy that had them paralyzed with fear. The enemy was a huge man named Goliath, three times the size of David, that was bullying the Israelites. But David didn't consider his small size. He saw a man that was not in covenant with his God and knew God was on their side. Unfortunately, the other soldiers didn't see it that way. They just saw the man's size. What did David do? He faced his giant and overpowered him with a small stone. This is your authority when in covenant with God. Face your giant and kill it with confidence you have in the keys Jesus delivered to you.

Deception is another weapon of our enemy. He can speak part truth, part lie. In India, there are millions and millions of gods that are worshipped. In all the stories of the origination of the main gods, there is a portion of God's truth in each one. But then those stories become quite out of line with scriptures in the Bible. Part truth, mostly deceit. If any part has a lie in it, then it's all wrong.

We can start believing things that are absolutely not true if we don't know the scripture. The bondage of our minds can be broken through the power of Jesus Christ and the Word. Reading the Bible, going to Bible studies with well-grounded teachers helps.

When you meet someone who is aware of their problem (their bondage), it is time to teach them. Again, help them understand God loves them right where they are. They don't have to get cleaned up to be accepted by God or to accept Jesus as their Lord and Savior. God and the Holy Spirit will take care of that in time.

What Happens When We Loose Heaven?

What you can do is to loose them from the bondage of the enemy. *Loose* is just the opposite of *bind* or *bound*. According to Webster's Dictionary, *loose* means "to free from a state of confinement or restraint." In Greek, it means "to break up, destroy, or dissolve." Sounds to me like we have been given permission to command Satan to release someone from bondage and dissolve those bonds.

Let me remind you, Satan is our enemy. He is not your friend. His only purpose is to kill you, steal from you, and destroy everything you desire in life. Jesus came to destroy the works of the enemy and to give us a life of abundance (1 John 3:8; John 10:10) There is no place in the mind of Christ for us to be without peace, joy, love of life, and moving steadily ahead to accomplish what God desires us to do in this life.

Jesus also declared to the Church (which means all who believe and received Jesus as Savior) that we can command that what is bound on earth will be bound in heaven and what is loosed on earth will be loosed in heaven.

I have read, meditated, and acted on those verses. We can think all day that Jesus gave us that kind of power, but until we declare and command with conviction using our voice, nothing will happen. All of heaven's angels are waiting for us to use the authority that Jesus declared to His children. He needs us to become His voice. You may ask, "How can we dare to be like Jesus?" Because He said to. Jesus had sacrificed Himself on the cross to become our sin, took on all our sicknesses and torments, then rose from the dead and, for forty days afterward, walked with the disciples to continue to teach.

When it was time for Him to leave and return to heaven, Jesus gave His last instructions. Jesus said, *"These signs **will** follow those who believe. In My name they **will** cast out demons; they **will** speak with new tongues; they **will** take up serpents; and if they drink anything deadly, it **will** by no means hurt them; they will lay hands on the sick, and they **will** recover"* (emphasis is mine).

Jesus could no longer be the only one with that power. He transferred His power and His authority to those who believed. Now, you and I carry that kind of authority. When we see or are ministering to someone who is trying to break out of their bondage, we can help. We can use our knowledge in the covenant we have with Almighty God, use the Name of Jesus, let the

Holy Spirit guide us as we demand Satan to loose his hold on a person that is bound up. In response, God will do what you have commanded.

There is no situation that is impossible. The only responsibility is for you to do what Jesus declared over to you. Jesus said in John 16:15, *"All things that the Father has are Mine. Therefore, I said that He will take of Mine and declare it to you."* You are now Jesus's hands and feet. You are His mouthpiece, and you have authority to help a person who is in bondage. You can make a difference. You can be the conduit between death and life for a person.

Ministering to Those in Bondage

There is no formula in which to minister. But there are some important points that need to be made. Let's say someone is in an addiction they know is destroying their peace, their future, and possibly their health. They must want help. If they aren't saved, now is a good time to get them saved. When they acknowledge that they know God can help, then the bondage of Satan must be broken. Declare that Satan has no authority over a child of God. Command Satan to release his hold, declare the spirit of addiction to be gone. Satan must cease and desist all maneuvers on their life.

It is important, at that time, to declare health, wholeness, and peace in their body. However, the spirit moves you, it is important to fill the void left by the demonic powers with the spirit of health, mental stability, wholeness, peace, or whatever is needed.

If someone has sickness in their body, speak to the parts of the body that need to be restored. For example, nerves, ligaments, muscles, bones, sound mind, any organ, or systems. Be specific then finally speak peace into their mind, soul, and body.

Always keep in mind, you are NOT the healer. Jesus, through you, is the Healer. If someone doesn't respond with healing, be assured you did what you were supposed to do. There can be many reasons people are not healed at that moment. They may be healed later that day or night. You may have activated healing, and it will be manifested in time. It may be that more teaching needs to be done or there is a generational curse that needs to be explored and dealt with. Don't let one incident dissuade you from ministering in the future.

All four gospels speak to unforgiveness. Bitterness, grudges, and unforgiveness can keep one from receiving the benefits we get as a child of God. Don't let those emotions provoked by the devil dominate you. Jesus said in Mark 11:25 and 26, *"And whenever you stand praying, if you have anything against anyone, forgive him that your Father in heaven may also forgive you your trespasses (sin). But if you do not forgive, neither will your Father in heaven forgive you."*

Jesus was adamant that one who holds unforgiveness must forgive. I know there are certain circumstances that seem impossible, but with God's help and that of the Holy Spirit, it will be possible.

When ministering and there is an immediate manifestation, you will see a profound difference in a person's countenance. In the beginning, they are tense, all out of sorts, and may be manifesting different negative emotions. After ministering, their countenance will be of one of total peace and tranquility. They often will remark that an incredible weight seems to have been lifted off them.

If there was a physical impairment that you prayed about, encourage them to do something they couldn't do before. It may have been a torn rotator cuff. Have them move their arm from the shoulder. If they had something with their leg or foot, get them to stand or walk. This is their step of faith and will build other's faith as well.

The first time I did this, I was surprised to see such incredible results. I shouldn't have been! God said it, I trusted His word and stepped out of my comfort zone. When the person declared they were changed, we all rejoiced. I can imagine the day Jesus was approached by the man with leprosy and asked if Jesus willed, would He (Jesus) heal him. Jesus said, "I am willing," and touched Him. The leper was immediately healed. I don't think there was one person present that wasn't smiling, laughing, and perhaps jumping with joy! I know, I would.

We must remember that God is a supernatural God. He does supernatural things. Supernatural means beyond what is natural. We must get into our mindset that God will do what He says. He is a God that does not lie (Heb. 6:18) .We live in a world that has taught us not to trust everything that is said, but in this case, God means what He says and says what He means. He is not a deceiver. He is always going to tell the truth. That is why you can step out when you have no doubt in your heart that you *can* move mountains.

"Have faith in God For assuredly I say to you, whoever says to this mountain, Be removed and be cast to the sea, and does not doubt in his heart, but believes that those things he says will be done, he will have whatever he says. Therefore I say to you, whatever things you ask when you pray, believe that you receive them, and you will have them." (Mark 11:23–24)

Mountains mentioned here doesn't mean a physical mountain. It means impossible circumstances in the natural sense. Bondages are mountains. Jesus said, "Have faith in God." Faith is more than believing, it is action. You can believe in your head all day long, but it isn't until you put action to your believing that you can call that faith. Speaking the Word is faith. Stepping out to help someone when you know it is God's will is faith.

Doubt and faith are complete opposites. Once I was able to get doubt out of my thinking, that's when I saw that God could use me. Doubt is questioning your ability. You can't think that way. God isn't looking for your ability, He is looking for your availability. If you are willing and don't doubt, then you will be an incredible vessel for God to work through.

Chapter 8

Conclusion

Now that you understand what the Keys of the Kingdom of Heaven are, you have the tools to live a life with more confidence. The keys have always been there, but knowing about them equips you for future battles and life skirmishes. Hosea 4:6 says, *"My people perish for lack of knowledge."* Without these keys, the enemy can take control over your mind, health, and life. But now, with these five keys, you can come out the victor.

The important factor is to remember the keys. They are all important, but the foundation key is your covenant with God. Nothing can separate you from your Master, Adonai. Yes, you can drift away from Him, but He will never leave you. His arms are always open to receive you. Ask for forgiveness and let Him back into your life.

Trust God

There are two principles in which you will be responsible in order for these keys to work. The first is TRUST. Believe it or not, God loves you more than you can possibly imagine.

He is bound to you spiritually whether you feel it or not. He is commited to you to succeed in life. He doesn't want you to "just hang in there" or "just hold on." He wants you to prosper. That means God, the designer and creator of the universe, wants you to continue to move ahead in your career, your family, your ideals, or your passions. He doesn't want you stuck in an endless rut of sickness and hopelessness.

In order to be all that God destined you to be, you need to build a relationship with Him. That means constant communion with Him. Reading His word, talking to Him, and most of all, listening to Him. Remember that voice in your inner being? That is God speaking to you through the Holy Spirit.

To trust God means that you have developed that relationship that is so close that you have no doubt that God will protect you, provide for you, fight for you, and open doors for you. Your confidence in your ability to help others through the Name of Jesus will make you a stronger child of God.

Finally, your life will be more at peace because you have that total confidence in your King, the Provider, Protector, and Healer. The trust you have in Him gives you more patience when things don't go the way you thought or in the time you imagined. He is in control of your life, and it is a good plan for you. His life for you is better than you could plan for or imagine.

Jeremiah 29:11 says: *For I know the thoughts that I think toward you, says the Lord, thoughts of peace and not of evil, to give you a future and a hope. Then you will call upon Me and go and pray to me and I will listen to you. And you will seek Me and find Me, when you search for Me with all your heart.*

Jesus said, *"The thief has come to steal, kill and destroy, but I have come that you may have life and live it abundantly"* (John

10:10). That word "abundantly" means "a superabundance, excessive, overflowing, surplus, more than enough." To me, that means He wants us to succeed and enjoy life in peace and prosperity.

Be Thankful

The second principle is thankfulness and gratitude. *"As you, therefore, have received Christ Jesus the Lord, so walk in Him rooted and built up in Him and established in the faith, as you have been taught, abounding in it with thanksgiving"* (Col. 2:6–7).

How can we possibly worship our God without a spirit of thankfulness? When we think of all the things He has helped us with, provided for us, protected us from, our hearts should be overflowing with thankfulness.

Then, when we are used by the Most High God to be a vessel in which someone's life is changed for the better, how much more should we celebrate and praise our God?

We can worship our Lord through music. Music is not man's invention. Music began in heaven with Lucifer as the worship leader. He led all the angels in worshipping God. Then when he felt he could lead or be better than God and rebelled. Lucifer was thrown out of heaven to the earth and became evil with the new name, Satan.

Music continues on earth today. Worship in churches all over the world is led by music. Music is the vehicle to tell of God's greatness and love so that people can meditate through music. Worship in church can be through rejoicing or humbling all for the purpose of realizing who God is, what Jesus did, and what He does for you today.

I personally have had incredible moments when I let the words of a song penetrate my very soul. One day, that happened where I couldn't stop saying, "Thank you Lord!" Over and over and over, I said it with all my heart. I believe it was that experience that moved me from believing in my head to believing with all my heart.

Fear Is Replaced with Confidence

With the five keys you have embraced, you will begin to realize you are walking through life with no fear. There are t-shirts that have emblazed on them, "No Fear." Every time I see that, I say to myself, "Yep, God's got me! He's got my back!"

Fear is Satan's number one weapon on humanity. If he can get us into a state of fear, whether through intimidation or a state of fear that immobilizes us, then he has won. Fear inhibits growth and with stunted growth, one cannot experience their full potential that God intended.

Imagine the new Christians in the years following Jesus's resurrection. There was a lot of persecution that could have kept them in so much fear that they would not have been able to spread the good news of the gospel of Jesus Christ. But we read that they had a confidence that their friends and coworkers didn't understand. Timothy was a young man who needed some confidence, so Paul wrote him, saying, "God has not given us a spirit of fear, but of power and of love and of a sound mind" (2 Timothy 1:7). We, too, have that same confidence. We have all the power Jesus had, a newfound love for humanity, and that sound mind is a mind that has been renewed with the word of God and has no more confusion and no more fear.

Do we expect God to hear and answer our petitions when we are doubtful? Jesus restored the Kingdom of Heaven back to the earth. Our confidence must be in what Jesus accomplished through His death and the regaining of the keys of the Kingdom and destroying the works of the devil. Through our understanding and confidence, we will see miracles again.

Are you ready to find confidence and peace as a child of God? Can you see yourself being used by God to minister to others?

Pray this prayer out loud:

I accept Jesus as my Savior and Lord. I place my life in His hands and want to be the best servant to the King of kings that I can. Forgive me for mistakes, offenses, or sins I have committed against you.

Father God, I want to use the keys you have left for me. I want to be bound to you in covenant, to know you will never leave me and I will never leave you.

Lord, I will confidently use the name of Jesus and the authority He delivered to me through His submission to the cross, defeating sin and death. With confidence, I will use my commanding power to speak the words to defeat the plans and strategies of the devil. I will declare and decree whatever You bind in heaven will be bound on earth, and whatever You loose in heaven will be loosed on earth.

Father, I can't do this in my own power. I need the baptism of the Holy Spirit in order to exercise my given right as an heir of God and joint heir of Jesus Christ with power and authority. Help me understand and comprehend your laws, statutes, and most of all, your love for me. I submit myself to you from now on.

I pray this in the mighty and holy Name of Jesus Christ, Amen.

CPSIA information can be obtained
at www.ICGtesting.com
Printed in the USA
BVHW041545280522
638357BV00001B/25